ARE YOU GOOD WITH GOD?

To my mom, Rita (Camacho) Horton,

the one who sowed the seeds of the G.O.S.P.E.L. in my heart as a child and prayed for me during my years of rebellion. Your legacy in Jesus will carry on not just through me but through every reader of this book. I can't wait to be reunited with you in glory, along with everyone else you led to Jesus.

Siempre te quiero mamá,

tu hijo, Damon

ARE YOU GOOD

D.A. HORTON

WITH GOD?

MOODY PUBLISHERS
CHICAGO

Scripture quotations are from the ESV® Bible (The Holy Bible, English Standard
Version®), Copyright © 2001 by Crossway, a publishing ministry of Good News
Publishers. Used by permission. All rights reserved.

Edited by Kevin Mungons
Interior design: Puckett Smartt
Cover design: Eleazar Ruiz
Author photo: RightNow Media

Library of Congress Cataloging-in-Publication Data
Names: Horton, D. A., author.
Title: Are you good with God? / D.A. Horton.
Description: Chicago : Moody Publishers, [2021] | Includes bibliographical
  references. | Summary: "Discover the surprising power of the
  G.O.S.P.E.L. story-explained as an acrostic by Pastor D. A. Horton. The
  gospel message is powerful, theological, and surprisingly simple to
  comprehend. Are You Good With God? explains giant truths so people from
  every background can understand"-- Provided by publisher.
Identifiers: LCCN 2021045597 (print) | LCCN 2021045598 (ebook) | ISBN
  9780802428707 | ISBN 9780802475183 (ebook)
Subjects: LCSH: Salvation--Christianity. | Bible. Genesis, I-III,
  1-8--Criticism, interpretation, etc. | Bible. Revelation XX,
  15-XXII--Criticism, interpretation, etc. | BISAC: RELIGION / Christian
  Ministry / Evangelism | RELIGION / Christian Living / General
Classification: LCC BT751.3 .H665 2021 (print) | LCC BT751.3 (ebook) |
  DDC 234--dc23
LC record available at https://lccn.loc.gov/2021045597
LC ebook record available at https://lccn.loc.gov/2021045598

Originally delivered by fleets of horse-drawn wagons, the affordable paperbacks
from D. L. Moody's publishing house resourced the church and served everyday
people. Now, after more than 125 years of publishing and ministry, Moody Publishers'
mission remains the same—even if our delivery systems have changed a bit.
For more information on other books (and resources) created from a biblical
perspective, go to www.moodypublishers.com or write to:

Moody Publishers
820 N. LaSalle Boulevard
Chicago, IL 60610

1 3 5 7 9 10 8 6 4 2

Printed in the United States of America

CONTENTS

Introduction: The Big Picture   9
The Bible 9
The Gospel 10

1. God's Design   19
God's Image 23
Open Fellowship 28

2. Our Downfall   33
Sin Introduced 34
Penalty and Price 39

3. God's Demonstration   47
Enter Jesus 48
Life Everlasting 55

4. Our Destination   63

Afterword 71
Notes 75

For I am not ashamed of the gospel, for it is the power of God for salvation to everyone who believes, to the Jew first and also to the Greek. For in it the righteousness of God is revealed from faith for faith, as it is written, "The righteous shall live by faith."

THE APOSTLE PAUL, IN ROMANS 1:16–17

THE BIG PICTURE

As soon as COVID-19 sent the world into lockdown, Netflix subscriptions went through the roof. By April 2020 there were 182 million Netflix subscribers globally. Sad to think, but more people are watching Netflix than reading their Bibles (and Bible reading actually declined by several percentage points during the pandemic).[1] If so, the rise of Netflix at least gives us the perfect backdrop for explaining how the Bible works.

THE BIBLE

Think of the Bible like a Netflix series. It's one story, God's story, told in four distinct seasons and fully unpacked in sixty-six episodes.

- Season One: God's Design (Genesis 1–2)
- Season Two: Our Downfall (Genesis 3:1–7)
- Season Three: God's Demonstration
  (Genesis 3:8–Revelation 20:15)
- Season Four: Our Destination
  (Revelation 21–22)

We will work through each of these seasons in this book. As with any story, the characters, plot (and plot twists), settings, and themes all help viewers follow along as the story unfolds. The same is true of the Bible. The cast is extensive. The plot movements and twists are not always rated PG. The settings are on location across three continents: Africa, Asia, and Europe. Yet, when it comes to the theme of the movie there is but one that exclusively traces the lead role's placement in the story. The lead role in God's story is Jesus. The theme tracing His placement is called *the gospel.* If you have a Bible, I encourage you to read each of the Scripture passages I mention here.

THE GOSPEL

In Romans 1:16–17 Paul says, "For I am not ashamed of the gospel, for it is the power of God for salvation to everyone who believes, to the Jew first and also to the Greek. For in it the righteousness of God is revealed from faith for faith, as it is written, 'The righteous shall live by faith.'"

Paul is simply saying that as a follower of Jesus, he is not embarrassed to share with others the theme that places Jesus as the lead role in God's story. Paul lists four reasons why he has no shame in doing this.

1. **The gospel carries the "power of God."** The Greek word for power in Paul's usage is *dynamis*. The inventors of the explosive called *dynamite* gave it that name because of the new substance's incredible power. It calls to mind the power and aftermath of an explosion. I think back to seeing the blast impact that took place downtown Beirut, Lebanon, in April 2020. Cellphone videos from people who were miles away captured the power of the blast, and pictures of the aftermath reveal the significant change in the terrain. There is no one who can deny the visible changes of downtown Beirut after experiencing this powerful explosion. Something even greater takes place in the life of a person who has experienced God's power. But rather than being destructive, it generates life. When the gospel is shared, God's unlimited power is put on display—He resurrects a dead soul by imparting eternal life. The changes seen in people's lives become undeniable to those who knew them before they encountered God's power, demonstrated through gospel sharing.

2. **The gospel carries God's power for "salvation"** for every type of person. God's power always has a purpose. His purpose for displaying His

power is revealed every time the gospel is shared. He extends salvation to humans by preventing them from facing the justice we deserve. The word salvation means to be delivered or rescued. We are not being saved from the devil or Satan, rather, the gospel saves us from the wrath of God, which is the just penalty and payment for our sins. When human beings sin, we rack up a debt that we're unable to pay in full. The gospel confronts this reality by showing us how God's story reveals a way for our sins to be paid off, so we can be debt free, and not face an eternal sentence in debtors' prison.

3. The gospel reveals the "righteousness of God."

The gospel describes God as being absolutely righteous, and His righteousness exposes the complete sinfulness of every human being. Since God is righteous, He cannot be in a relationship with anyone who is not completely righteous. This means the entire human race has been separated from the God who created us. This separation is not because of our culture, ethnicity, gender, primary language, or social class—it is because of our sinfulness or unrighteousness. The gospel explains how *all* sinners can be declared to be and made absolutely righteous by God, so we can be brought back into a

right relationship with Him throughout all of
eternity!

4. **The gospel transcends ethnicity, culture, gender, and social class** because it's "from faith for
faith." The meaning of "from faith for faith" puts
an individual focus on one person's faith to
another person's faith. When the gospel is
shared, God individually nuances His truth
so the individual who is processing it comprehends it, then embraces Jesus as the focus of
the gospel. Every individual reading this book
has a story. Your story is important, and it's
still being written. The gospel is the bridge that
connects our story to God's story! It allows
each of us to interact with the lead role (Jesus)
on a personal level, and accept His offer to play
a supporting cast role!

I'm going to share a spoiler right now. There is
a way to identify the theme of the gospel early on in
the Bible, so you won't miss it through our journey
together in this book. Similar to how film director
M. Night Shyamalan used the color red to symbolize important nuances in *The Sixth Sense* (if you
never noticed that until reading this, I guess I'm
sharing two spoilers), I want to clue you in to some
important subthemes that help us see the gospel as

the major theme of God's story. I'll do this by turning G.O.S.P.E.L. into the following acronym:

G — God's Image

O — Open Fellowship

S — Sin Introduced

P — Penalty and Price

E — Enter Jesus

L — Life Everlasting

WHAT IS THE GOSPEL?

GOD'S DESIGN → OUR DOWNFALL

OPEN FELLOWSHIP

- Genesis 1:26–27
- Every human bears "God's image"

- Genesis 1–2
  At one point in human history there was no abuse, addictions, broken families, depression, suicide, or death.

- Genesis 3:1–7
  The Fall of Humanity

- Romans 5:12
  Sin spread to the entire human race

GOD'S IMAGE

SIN INTRODUCED

Before we move on, take a look at this visual below to see how the Bible and its four seasons align with the breakdown of the acronym G.O.S.P.E.L.

GOD'S DEMONSTRATION

OUR DESTINATION

PENALTY & PRICE

- The penalty for sin is death
- The price for sin is the shedding of blood from an unblemished sacrifice

- John 1:1–4
  Jesus is fully God and added full humanity to His deity
- Matthew 20:28
  Jesus came to die in the place of sinners
- Jesus resurrected!

ENTER JESUS

LIFE EVERLASTING

- Jesus offers life eternal to anyone no matter ethnicity, gender, or social class
- John 17:3 defines "eternal life"

Then God said, "Let us make man in our image, after our likeness. And let them have dominion over the fish of the sea and over the birds of the heavens and over the livestock and over all the earth and over every creeping thing that creeps on the earth." So God created man in his own image, in the image of God he created him; male and female he created them.

GENESIS 1:26–27

1

GOD'S DESIGN

God's story opens by framing how He designed creation. Genesis 1:1 says, "In the beginning God created the heavens and the earth." We can't overlook some truths in this statement. First, the Bible is not a book that is begging the reader to believe God exists. Second Timothy 3:16–17 says God is the one who revealed His story as recorded in the Bible, the fact that the Bible exists. This fact should lead readers to believe God exists. When I send my wife a text message, I don't have to prove to her that I exist. The fact I texted her is evidence enough that I'm alive and communicating to her through my text message. The Bible is similar to Him texting us, sharing with us insights about His story.

The idea that God does not exist is a modern phenomenon that has only been popular a couple hundred years. Throughout human history cultures, ethnicities, and people groups all over the world had a belief in one or many supreme beings who ruled over them. This truth is supported by Ecclesiastes 3:11: "He has made everything beautiful in its time. Also, he has put eternity into man's heart, yet so that he cannot find out what God has done from the beginning to the end." Solomon, the writer of this passage, says God has put in every heart a desire to understand what our existence and work means. We know there is something and/ or someone beyond us who is eternal. In our life, we strive to please the One who is eternal and gives us meaning for living—this someone is God.

The prophet Jeremiah testified that "the LORD is the true God; he is the living God and the everlasting King" (Jeremiah 10:10). The Psalms declare that "his understanding is beyond measure" (Psalm 147:5). But because of our sin, instead of pursuing the only True and Living God who cannot be fully understood, we often create gods that we can understand and even control. When these false gods no longer quench our quest for the eternal, there are times we conclude an eternal God must not exist. However, we must realize that we're arrogant to come to such a conclusion without exhaustively (or totally) examining all the evidence. It is impossible for one human mind to possess all the knowledge that has ever existed, is existing, and will exist in the future. No one person can say they have examined all of knowledge in order to then determine no god exists. A total embrace of all knowledge will always be outside of the grasp of humans. When people say there is no god, they have simply stopped being diligent in their research, rather than accepting God's claim as being full of truth.

Romans 1:18–23 informs us how God's existence is made evident every time we connect with the nature that He created. One way to understand this natural evidence of God's existence is to look at the clothes we wear, the shoes we put on, and even the electronic devices we use regularly. Before we purchased them, they were an idea in someone's mind. This idea was shared, and a design was created. The design was given a brand, mass produced, and then sold to consumers. Every design has a designer. Nature is no different, and God's story reveals Him to be the designer of all of creation.

Another evidence is the idea of morality, what is right and wrong. Our society gives an inconsistent definition of right and wrong. Often people think they have the right to determine what is right and wrong for themselves. This leads us to believe that everyone has the right to claim what is true to them. And where there is disagreement, no one is either right or wrong, because it's "their truth" they are believing.

This confusion grows out of an idea that says there is no such thing as an absolute truth. Some say truth is fluid and changes because it's subjective, in contrast to being concrete, objective, and eternally stable. But if truth is always changing, and this is what prevents it from being absolute, then the very claim "there is no such thing as absolute truth" has defeated itself because it can't be true. If this statement is not true, then it reveals truth is objective not subjective. If truth then is objective, we can truly find an acceptable definition to the question of morality, which is "what is right and wrong?"

If humanity believes the lie that there is no objective standard for defining right and wrong, then working toward any form of justice makes no sense. Also, if there is no god, and we are truly in a process of human evolution, then why should humanity help any victims of abuse, displaced populations due to the horrors of genocide and war, or feed the hungry? If there is no god, then why are we fighting against nature's way of removing the weak so the strong will be those who survive?

Humans work to help marginalized and vulnerable people because we truly realize we have compassion and empathy. These characteristics came from somewhere, which we'll identify in a moment. As we look back to the issue of morality,

God's story unpacks how there is both absolute truth and a concrete definition of right and wrong. Since God is the source of righteousness, we should read His story to see what He classifies as right and wrong behaviors. Every human being has been given the ability to determine right from wrong because we are all equally made in God's image.

GOD'S IMAGE

- Genesis 1:26–27
- Every human bears "God's image"

GOD'S IMAGE

The gospel theme is first introduced to readers in Genesis 1:26–27: "Then God said, 'Let us make man in our image, after our likeness. And let them have dominion over the fish of the sea and over the birds of the heavens and over the livestock and over all the earth and over every creeping thing that creeps on the earth.' So God created man in his own image, in the image of God he created him; male and female he created them."

It's important we start any conversation about the gospel with God's creation of humanity. God's story reveals early on how He made every man and woman in His image. There are a couple of truths we need to identify here as it relates to God's design.

First, there is one human race. The idea of there being many races on planet earth is something not found in God's story—it is a human idea that traces back to the colonization of the Americas.[2] Within our one human race are numerous beautiful ethnicities, giving distinction among civilizations, languages, and people groups around the world. God's story traces the ancestral roots of our one human race back to one common set of parents, Adam and Eve (see Genesis 3:20 and Acts 17:23–26). The gospel confronts classism, racism, sexism, and xenophobia head-on by showing an equality among the entire human race. All these vices exist because sinful human beings, who were in positions of decision-making, showed partiality (or favoritism) to others like them, and built walls of segregation among humans. All this was done outside of God's design for humanity.

Second, humans have unique characteristics. Being created in God's image does not mean humans are part God and part human. Neither does it mean we will become equal with God as we progress over time. Since John 4:24 says God is spirit, and since a spirit is immaterial, then being made in the image of God requires us to understand the uniqueness of humanity when compared to every other type of God's creation. We discover our uniqueness when we list the immaterial characteristics (or attributes) that God shared with humans alone. Here are some examples of the characteristics He shared with us:

- **Emotions**—Through God's story He reveals emotional expressions that we as humans also express. Such emotions as anger (Psalm 106:40), compassion (Exodus 33:19), grief (Isaiah 63:10), hate (Psalm 5:5), joy (Nehemiah 8:10), and of course love (Psalm 136).

- **Morality**—The ability to determine what is right and wrong.

- **Personality**—The ability to express individuality through behavior.

- **Rationality**—The ability to assess and process information.

- **Spirituality**—The ability for our soul to exist. Genesis 2:7 says, "then the LORD God formed the man of dust from the ground and breathed into his nostrils the breath of life, and the man became a living creature." God breathed a singular breath into the first human He created, described by the Hebrew phrase *of life*, a plural word meaning Adam was brought to life both physically and spiritually. The soul of every human continues to live after physical death takes place (see Luke 16:19–31).

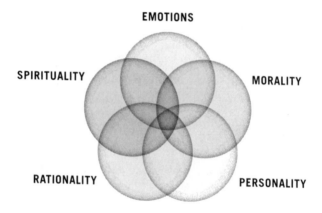

By giving humanity these attributes, God equipped Adam and Eve to walk in obedience, multiply the human race, and creatively manage nature. Here's a flashback to Genesis 2. The setting is in the garden of Eden, before God created Eve. In Genesis 2:15–17 God made a covenant with Adam saying that if he obeyed God by managing the Garden of Eden and eating from every tree in the garden except the tree of knowledge of good and evil, then Adam could keep living in the garden. However, if Adam disobeyed God's covenant by eating from the tree of knowledge of good and evil, Adam would die.

Then comes the first time in God's story that He said something was not good—man was alone. As the man was naming every animal, he noticed that each animal he named had an equal mate of its kind. Adam realized he didn't have an equal mate who shared his humanity. Genesis 2:21–22 says, "So the LORD God caused a deep sleep to fall upon the man, and while he slept took one of his ribs and closed up its place with flesh. And the rib that the LORD God had taken from the man he made into a woman and brought her to the man." The rib's position amplifies God's design for closeness, cooperation, and intimacy between man and woman.

For the next part of the story, cue up the Etta James classic, "At Last," where "my lonely days are over and life is like a song."

When the man woke up, God presented the woman to him, and he rejoiced. He finally found the equal mate he was looking for! What we witness here is God's design for the covenant of marriage. For humanity to flourish and walk in obedience to the covenant God made with Adam, he and his bride were to work together for the rest of their lives. We see God intended for marriage to be between one man and one woman, resulting in a lifetime of teamwork as they walk in obedience to God.

OPEN FELLOWSHIP

OPEN FELLOWSHIP

- Genesis 1–2
At one point in human history there was no abuse, addictions, broken families, depression, suicide, or death.

At this point in human history, God enjoyed open fellowship with the entire human race— Adam and Eve. It's important to understand that there was no animosity, distrust, or hostility between God and humanity, and the same was true of the relationship between Adam and Eve. Take a minute to consider Genesis 2:24–25: "Therefore a man shall leave his father and his mother and hold fast to his wife, and they shall become one flesh. And the man and his wife were both naked and were not ashamed." Moses wrote this passage about Israel's wandering in the wilderness before entering the promised land. He introduced Israel to the high priority of the marriage relationship. At the same time, Moses shed light on the fact that both Adam and Eve were naked, and they had no shame. This phrase is not talking about the lack of insecurity regarding our personal physique. Rather, it is platforming how Adam and Eve had no fear of being exposed, because neither of them were living a secret life.

In this time of human history there was no such thing as baby-momma or baby-daddy drama. Adam wasn't sliding into anyone's direct messages, and Eve wasn't up late at night on Tinder. During this time there was no such thing as abuse or molestation. There were no addictions or chemical dependencies. No broken families, and fatherlessness didn't exist. No one had ever committed suicide, no one turned to self-mutilation, and no one had ever experienced death. God's design for His creation did not include any of these realities that are in our world today. So what happened?

Then the LORD God said, "Behold, the man has become like one of us in knowing good and evil. Now, lest he reach out his hand and take also of the tree of life and eat, and live forever—" therefore the LORD God sent him out from the garden of Eden to work the ground from which he was taken. He drove out the man, and at the east of the garden of Eden he placed the cherubim and a flaming sword that turned every way to guard the way to the tree of life.

MOSES, IN GENESIS 3:22–24

2

OUR DOWNFALL

We are not sure how long God's design for humanity and open fellowship was enjoyed by God, Adam, and Eve. As God's story continues, we are given clear insight as to how the downfall of the human race took place. Consider that we have never experienced life before the downfall of humanity. We read God's story through our lens of experience, where death happens to children in the womb, disease runs rampant, and it is normal to doubt the truthfulness of God's Word. All of these nuances were not the case in the garden of Eden, so we must take this into consideration as we read further in God's story.

SIN INTRODUCED

- Genesis 3:1–7
  The Fall of Humanity
- Romans 5:12
  Sin spread to the entire
  human race

**SIN
INTRODUCED**

Genesis 3:1–19 is the plot twist I've been preparing you for. Here we read about a serpent (spoiler alert) who is the antagonist in God's story, disguised as a creature Eve would've been familiar with. Later in God's story Satan is called the "ancient serpent" (Revelation 20:2), and Jesus calls him the "father of lies" (John 8:44). Satan is an intelligible being who can talk. In Genesis 3 a talking snake sounds like mythological fiction, but it is Satan, who took the form of an animal.

Focus on the strategy of deception that Satan used to deceive Eve. This is crucial to understand because Satan uses this same trickery to this day.

1. **Satan planted a seed of doubt in Eve's mind** by asking a question: "Did God actually say . . . ?" His question was not one looking for a direct

answer—he was trying to get Eve to second-guess what God said.

2. **Satan gave Eve space to answer.** If she responded now, a conversation could start. The longer they talked, Satan could continue to sow more seeds of doubt and deception. Eve took the bait and responded by saying, "We may eat of the fruit of the trees in the garden, but God said, 'You shall not eat of the fruit of the tree that is in the midst of the garden, neither shall you touch it, lest you die.'" Her subtle misquote is hard to catch, but Eve added to God's command by saying "neither shall you touch it, lest you die." She added something God did not say and framed Him as being overbearing and unfair. Satan picked up on this little nuance and exploited it!

3. **Satan tempted Eve to doubt God's goodness.** He did so by saying, "You will not surely die. For God knows that when you eat of it your eyes will be opened, and you will be like God, knowing good and evil." Satan frames God as one who is holding something back from Eve. His goal is to get her thinking, "if God was truly good to me, He would've given me all that He has . . . including knowledge of good and evil!"

4. Satan stepped back and left Eve with her confused thoughts, which were not based on an accurate understanding of God's word (what He said) and God's character (that He is perfectly good). Through this deceived lens, she looked at the fruit from the tree of knowledge of good and evil and saw it in a new light.

SATAN'S STRATEGY OF DECEIT

Sow doubt about God's word → Give us space to respond to Him → Tempt us to doubt God's goodness → Step back and let us see an opportunity to sin

What comes next is a chain of events that turned our entire world upside down. Eve saw the fruit was food ("desires of the flesh"), it looked good ("desires of the eyes"), and by eating it she would gain wisdom she didn't have before ("pride of life"). She touched the fruit, took it, and ate it. Then she gave it to Adam—who was with her! Don't miss this. Adam was there, but did not speak up to remind his bride about the truth of God's word. Adam was not deceived—he hadn't been engaging with Satan—so Adam's action of taking and eating the fruit was pure disobedience to God's command. Just like that, in the blink of an eye, Adam broke his covenant with God.

Open fellowship with God and each other was lost. Romans 5:12 says that in this moment sin and death entered into our human race through Adam's disobedience. The entire human race was both relationally separated from God and spiritually dead. Remember, when God breathed the breath of life it was plural, so although Adam did not physically die after eating the fruit, his countdown to physical death now began. However, in this moment, spiritually Adam and his bride did die.

Since all of humanity traces our ancestral roots back to Adam and Eve, Romans 5:12–21 says every human has inherited relational separation from God, a sinful nature, and spiritual death. Psalm 51:5 asserts that while we were being formed in our mother's womb, sin was already present inside of us because each of us has inherited from our parents, who inherited it from theirs, and so forth all the way back to Adam and Eve. Psalm 58:3 clues us in to the fact since we are wicked, we are prone to lie because lying is a sin and sin has infected our entire nature. Jesus says in John 8:34, "Truly, truly, I say to you, everyone who practices sin is a slave to sin." We must understand that not only have we inherited sin we naturally practice it, and if we have committed even one sin, which every human has, then we are slaves to sin. Our sinful desires are lord and master over every single one of us.

Last, Paul says in Ephesians 2:1–3, "And you were dead in the trespasses and sins in which you once walked, following the course of this world, following the prince of the power of the air, the spirit that is now at work in the sons of disobedience—among whom we all once lived in the passions of our flesh, carrying out the desires of the body and the mind, and were by nature children of wrath, like the rest of mankind." Here Paul confirms that every human, although physically alive, is spiritually dead. Death means to be separated from life. If we are spiritually dead, we are relationally separated from God, the source of life. In addition, Satan influences people in positions of power to create structures and systems that allow them to rule over other people in sinful ways. These sinful power structures prevent people from seeking God for freedom from sin's slavery.

To provide humanity with a solution, God made a covenant with Israel, calling on them to obey God's system of laws. In Leviticus 11:44 God says that since He is absolutely holy, anyone in a relationship with Him must be absolutely holy too. If Israel was to be relationally connected to God, they would need a solution to the penalty and price that accompanies sin.

PENALTY & PRICE

PENALTY & PRICE

- The penalty for sin is death
- The price for sin is the shedding of blood from an unblemished sacrifice

Sin comes with a penalty and a price. The penalty is death, and the price is shed blood from a pure sacrifice who dies in the place of the sinner. As we continue reading God's story, Genesis 3:8–24 highlights how God uncovered Adam and Eve's disobedience. The story tells how God extended them mercy as a reinforcement of His just and righteous character. As soon as Adam ate the fruit, he and Eve realized they were naked. They lost their innocence and now feared being exposed. They tried to hide what they did by taking leaves and sewing them together to cover their nakedness, which was now their shame. Then they heard God walking through the garden, which was typical, but for the first time in their lives they felt guilt in addition to their new emotional struggle with shame.

God called out for Adam, who was hiding and scared to see God. Adam told God that he realized he was naked, so he ran to hide. God asked Adam if he ate the fruit that God had commanded him not to eat. Rather than taking ownership of his sin, Adam threw his bride under the bus, and even tried to toss blame on God, the one who gave him his bride!

God confronted Eve, and she passed the blame on to the serpent. God then pronounced a curse on the serpent, Eve, Adam, and all of nature. In Genesis 3:15 we read the first hint of Jesus entering in God's story: "he shall bruise your head, and you shall bruise his heel." The serpent would go on to bruise the head of the offspring of the woman—Jesus— who would ultimately crush the serpent's head!

God could've put Adam and Eve to death physically, but He showed them mercy instead. *Mercy* means to withhold a required punishment. God's mercy is seen in Genesis 3:21 when He clothed Adam and Eve in garments made of animal skins. Here's what we can't miss: since God is just, He had to deal with Adam and Eve's sin, including the penalty and price that comes with it. The penalty is death, and the price is shed blood from a pure sacrifice who dies in the place of the sinner. The animals died in Adam and Eve's place. They were physically covered by garments given to them by God, and the stain of their sin was covered by the blood of the animals that died. Adam and Eve's first attempt to clothe themselves was insufficient in the eyes of God. In order for sinners to have the guilt and shame of their sins properly covered, it must be done in obedience to God's instructions, not man's opinions or thoughts.

Romans 6:23 says, "For the wages of sin is death, but the free gift of God is eternal life in Christ Jesus our Lord." Let's think about that word *wages*. It should remind us of how the company we work for should pay us. Growing up, my family lived from paycheck to paycheck. Every payday my dad would calculate his hours at our dinner table. More than a few times my dad's check was short, and he would return to his employer asking to be paid the missing amount. My dad had every right to express this to his employer, because they agreed on a certain hourly wage for every hour he worked. He wasn't looking for a handout—he was asking for what was owed to him.

Romans 6:23 also reminds me of a 401(k) retirement plan. When someone takes part of their paycheck and puts it into a retirement account, it grows compounding interest over time. When they retire, they receive monthly distributions from that account for the rest of their life. Since all of humanity is born in sin, dead in sin, and slaves to sin, we are rightfully owed eternal death, which is eternal conscious separation from God. This is not just physical death. It is eternal spiritual death that is paid out in distributions like a 401(k) retirement plan. Every day we live outside of a relationship with God, we are making contributions of sin that are stored up, and later distributed to us throughout an eternity of punishment. But God provides a better way!

As part of the law that God gave Israel, He set up a sacrificial system (Leviticus 1–7) to provide atonement for the sins of His people. The word *atonement* simply means to cover. Through this sacrificial system, God covered the stain that sin left on His people's hearts. This is similar to a person who owns a white couch, and to keep it clean they cover it with plastic. Think what happens if someone removes the plastic and spills Cherry Kool-Aid. You could to scrub the stain forever, but all you would accomplish is changing the color from bright red to pink.

The owner of the couch sees the stain and places the plastic back over the couch to cover the stain. However, the stain can still be seen through the plastic. The owner of the couch decides to buy a blanket to put on top of the plastic, preventing the stain from being seen. This is what God's sacrificial system accomplished for Israel on the Day of Atonement. Sin's stain was not removed, only covered temporarily. There's still a need to remove the penalty and price for sin, as well as the stain it leaves on the hearts of humans. Hebrews 9:22 says, "Indeed, under the law almost everything is purified with blood, and without the shedding of blood there is no forgiveness of sins." Here God again explains that the only acceptable payment for the price of sin is shed blood from a pure sacrifice that dies in the place of the sinner. At this point in God's story, we see how the entire human race is in dire need.

For while we were still weak, at the right time Christ died for the ungodly. For one will scarcely die for a righteous person— though perhaps for a good person one would dare even to die—but God shows his love for us in that while we were still sinners, Christ died for us.

THE APOSTLE PAUL, IN ROMANS 5:6–8

3

GOD'S DEMONSTRATION

We have now arrived at the portion of God's story where the lead role is fully revealed. The timing of God's plan to reveal His lead role was accompanied by the setting of a global stage. Prior to the lead role's entrance, much of the world was familiar with a specific type of Greek that was common due to Alexander the Great's spreading Greek culture and language in the lands he conquered. This historic platform sets up the reading of Paul in Galatians 4:4–5 where he says, "But when the fullness of time had come, God sent forth his Son, born of woman, born under the law, to redeem those who were under the law, so that we might receive adoption as sons."

ENTER JESUS

- John 1:1–4
  Jesus is fully God and added
  full humanity to His deity
- Matthew 20:28
  Jesus came to die in the
  place of sinners
- Jesus resurrected!

**ENTER
JESUS**

John 1:1 says, "In the beginning was the Word,
. . . and the Word was God." John prepares the readers of God's story and helps them see the unique
role Jesus has in God's story. John is saying Jesus
is eternally God, as well as equal with God, and
essentially God. Jesus cannot be reduced to being
a good teacher, prophet, or a moral person. Jesus
is fully God, and as John continues to verse 14, he
bears witness to Jesus, adding full humanity to His
full deity. Jesus invaded our world on a mission.
His mission is communicated by another eyewit-
ness to His life, Matthew. In Matthew 20:28 it says,
"Even as the Son of Man came not to be served but
to serve, and to give his life as a ransom for many."
The word *for* in Matthew 20:28 is a reference to
someone doing something in the place of another

person. The word *ransom* is a financial term that was used to buy slaves out of the debt of their slavery.

These nuances help us understand, then, that the reason for Jesus entering into God's story as the lead role in this moment in history was to be the unblemished sacrifice that died in the place of sinful human beings. In order for Jesus' payment to be accepted by God for the price of sin, Jesus needed to live an absolutely perfect life. The measurement of perfection was the law God gave the Israelites, which included 613 laws. No human being ever has been able to live out, in sinless perfection, all 613 laws. Anyone can claim to have lived out the law perfectly; however, the test for this would be Jesus' death.

One evening a few days before Christmas, my wife, Elicia, asked if I could go to Target for a few items she needed for Christmas dinner. When our son, Duce, heard I was going to Target, he ran into the room and asked if he could come with me. Duce normally asked for us to buy him Legos each time we went to Target. However, this time, it was different. Duce wanted to buy himself a box of Legos because he had money.

Elicia and I looked at each other in disbelief, but Duce was only four years old. Where would he get money from? I asked him if he really had money and he said he did. So I told him to put on his Batman slippers and he could come with me.

Soon I had picked up everything on Elicia's list and was ready to check out, when Duce reminded me he was going to buy himself Legos. Still in a state of disbelief, I let him continue to think he was going to purchase his own Legos. He picked up a box that cost over $60.00. I asked him again, "Are you sure you can pay for this?" Impatiently, he assured me he could. "Let's check out and go home," he added.

When it was our turn at the cashier, I unloaded our basket and purposely set the box of Legos at the end. The cashier noticed the large box and asked Duce, "Is your daddy buying your Christmas present early?" Duce answered, "No, I'm buying this. I have the money." The cashier looked at me, surprised. By this time, I'd had enough of the game. In Jerry Maguire fashion, I said, "Show me the money!"

Duce reached into his pocket and pulled out a wad of crumpled up papers that were dollar bills from the replica Target checkout stand we had bought him last Christmas!

At that moment, it hit me. Duce thought that because his money worked when we played with this pretend Target checkout, it would work in the real Target. My heart sank, knowing I had to tell Duce the truth—this money was not real. Not

Target or any other real store could accept play money for his purchase of Legos.

Duce was confused but before he could have a meltdown, I told him I would help him out. I asked the cashier to add his Lego box to the bill. Then I explained the following to Duce:

1. The cashier would tell me the total amount of payment due

2. I would insert my debit card into the machine so I could attempt to make the payment in full

3. The machine began to read my card, and that is when, electronically, Target told my bank how much I owed and my bank responded by sending the exact amount required, in the only acceptable form of payment Target would take, US dollars

4. If my payment was accepted, a word would pop up on the screen and we would know if my payment was accepted or rejected

When I was done explaining this process to Duce, the cashier announced the total. I put my debit card in the machine to read my chip and we waited. In those few moments my son's eyes were glued to the cashier's screen. And then it happened—a word appeared. It was not one of my son's sight words, so he immediately looked at me to read the word and explain what it meant.

"Duce, the word is 'approved,' and that means my payment was accepted," I said.

Right after I said this, a piece of paper printed out of the cash register, and I asked my son, "Duce, what do we call that piece of paper?"

"A receipt," he replied.

I told my son he was absolutely right, and on the receipt was printed every item that I paid for in full. I told him the items used to belong to a Target store, but since I have paid for them, now they rightfully belong to me. I told him we could walk out of the store and nobody could say we stole any of these items because I paid for them, and they will go wherever I want to take them.

When we got home my son told his mom about

everything that happened, and that's when I gave him the box of Legos as a gift. Remember—he thought he had an acceptable form of payment to buy the Legos, only to realize that his payment was not acceptable. So I was able to pay the amount owed with the acceptable form of payment, and now I was choosing to give him the Legos as a gift. He couldn't buy them himself, and he couldn't work to earn them. All he could do was receive them as the gift that I intended.

This story mirrors what Jesus did. Bible verses such as 2 Corinthians 5:21, Hebrews 7:26, and 1 Peter 2:22 all point to Jesus' sinless life. He never broke one of God's laws. When Jesus went to the cross, He did so in the place of human sinners. While Jesus was on the cross, He absorbed the entire eternal debt that sinful humans racked up. Here we must understand a vital truth. The debt for sin is eternal. Since human beings are created, we are by definition *finite*, the opposite of being eternal. It is impossible for us, as finite humans, to pay an eternal debt. To think we can accomplish this is just as foolish as my telling you I can fit the total volume of the Pacific ocean (which spans 63.8 million square miles) into a 32 oz. cup. The cup cannot contain the entire volume of the ocean—rather, the ocean would consume and drown the cup.

In a similar way, if the volume of water represents our sin debt, it is larger than all the oceans and bodies of water on earth. If we are the cup (because of our finite limitations), there's no possible way we can absorb our debt. We become absorbed by it! This is where Jesus, who is eternal, went to the cross and became like a sponge, absorbing our debt down to the last drop in the few hours He was on the cross. After Jesus surrendered His life He was buried for three days. The universe waited to see if His payment was received by God. The Bible reports the historical fact of Jesus' resurrection, seen by multiple eyewitnesses (Matthew 28, Mark 16, Luke 21–24, and John 20). When Jesus rose out of the grave, that was God the Father telling the universe, "Approved!" God accepted the perfect payment of Jesus' shed blood in the place of sinners.

LIFE EVERLASTING

> ### LIFE EVERLASTING
>
> - Jesus offers life eternal to anyone no matter ethnicity, gender, or social class
> - John 17:3 defines "eternal life"

Now this is where God's story has another plot twist. Since Jesus' resurrection is real, sinners from every ethnicity, gender, and social class who hear the gospel account can take the plea bargain God offers them through Jesus. We can have our sin debt forgiven, and the stain of sin removed from our heart! You may be asking, "A plea bargain?" Yes, a plea bargain.

In the American judicial system, a plea bargain is offered to an offender when the prosecutor has a strong case. The prosecutor negotiates a deal with the offender so the case won't have to go to trial.[3] If the offender pleads guilty to the lesser charges, they can receive a lighter sentence. But if the offender rejects the plea bargain and the case goes to trial, they can be found guilty of the full charges pressed upon them. They will be sentenced in accordance with what is required to bring forth justice.

The plea bargain God offers is similar, yet there's some distinction we must examine. Since all of humanity is already guilty of sin, and because God is absolutely just, He is not negotiating with lesser charges. Instead, God's plea bargain involves the Judge Himself—Jesus—who stepped from His judicial bench and took the full death sentence in the place of sinners (see John 5:22–23 and Revelation 20:11–15). When Jesus rose from the grave, the execution sentence was still paid in full!

Human sinners can embrace the following plea bargain God offers, and it is as simple as A-B-C:

- **Admit** you are guilty of all your sins. **Ask** Jesus to forgive you and apply His shed blood to your sin debt to have it washed away. "For all have sinned and fall short of the glory of God" (Romans 3:23).

- **Believe** in what Jesus has done to take your place on the cross and endured your sentence. "For God so loved the world, that he gave his only Son, that whoever believes in him should not perish but have eternal life" (John 3:16).

- **Confess** your belief in Jesus' resurrection, which allowed God to remove the complete rap sheet of sin from your account. "If you confess with your mouth that Jesus is Lord and believe in your heart that God raised him from the dead, you will be saved" (Romans 10:9).

GOD'S PLEA BARGAIN

Acknowledge you're guilty of all your sins

Believe in what Jesus has done

Confess your belief in Jesus' resurrection

The plea bargain God offers includes the gift of life everlasting from Jesus. *Life everlasting* is defined in John 17:3: "And this is eternal life, that they know you, the only true God, and Jesus Christ whom you have sent." To possess eternal life means to hear the gospel, embrace Jesus, and know Him personally as your Savior. Paul says in 2 Corinthians 5:20 that the role of those who have been saved by Jesus is to make the gospel known. Sinful humans from every ethnicity, gender, and social class can be reconciled to God through Jesus Christ.

To be reconciled means to have a fully restored relationship. Remember earlier in God's story when Adam and Eve had a right relationship with God?

Well, since all humans trace our roots back to Adam and Eve, this means all humans (everywhere in the world) can hear the gospel and embrace Jesus by taking God's plea bargain. Everyone who does this will be brought back into open fellowship with God!

Here's another amazing nuance of the gospel. When sinners embrace Jesus, not only do they have their sins forgiven, they are eternally declared "not guilty" by God Himself. This is because the perfect life of Jesus has been given to them, to replace their rap sheet. When the sin debt was forgiven, God didn't leave the account with a $0 balance. God does something amazing! He applies an infinite amount of righteousness—just like a cash app, applied directly to the person who just embraced Jesus (Romans 4–5).

Then I saw a new heaven and a new earth, for the first heaven and the first earth had passed away, and the sea was no more. And I saw the holy city, new Jerusalem, coming down out of heaven from God, prepared as a bride adorned for her husband. And I heard a loud voice from the throne saying, "Behold, the dwelling place of God is with man. He will dwell with them, and they will be his people, and God himself will be with them as their God. He will wipe away every tear from their eyes, and death shall be no more, neither shall there be mourning, nor crying, nor pain anymore, for the former things have passed away."

THE APOSTLE JOHN, IN REVELATION 21:1–4

4

OUR DESTINATION

God's story ends with the design that He introduced in the beginning, but was lost through Adam's sin. Now His story is being fully restored because of Jesus' perfect obedience! Everyone who has heard the gospel and embraced Jesus as their Savior gains citizenship into the city of God, described in Revelation 21–22. In the city of God, life returns to the perfection that God planned for the garden of Eden—no abuse, death, or sin—a perfect life in eternity for those who embraced Jesus.

God's story ends very differently for those who reject God's plea bargain. As we learn in Revelation 20, they are given what is justly due to them. For the rest of eternity they pay out of the wages of their sin, separated from God in the lake of fire. Since God is just, He can't overlook the penalty and price for sin. This is why it is important for everyone who has taken the plea bargain God offers to make as many people aware of it as possible, so they too can be saved from enduring God's wrath poured out on them for all eternity.

The location of your destination is up to you. "The Lord is not slow to fulfill his promise as some count slowness, but is patient toward you, not wishing that any should perish, but that all should reach repentance" (2 Peter 3:9). This passage means God has provided with you this opportunity to turn away from your sins and accept the plea bargain He offers through Jesus. *It is never too late.* As long as you have breath in your lungs, God is offering you an opportunity to hear the gospel, repent (turn from your way of life), and by faith embrace Jesus.

I remember a time when a friend of mine and I were walking down the street on a hot August day in Kansas City. We wanted to share the gospel with anyone we met on the street. But because it was hot and humid, no one was out. We got hungry and wanted to stop at a storefront taco spot. When we tried to open the door, we realized the place was closed. We began to walk away when we heard someone yell out, "Hey! Who you looking for?" We turned around and noticed a man with brown corduroy pants, no shirt, and a scruffy beard. He held a brown bag with a tall can of beer inside.

I yelled back, "We're good, bro!" before my friend and I turned our backs on him to walk back to church. A few seconds later we heard the same man yell again, "Hey! Who you looking for?" I turned around again and told him the same thing I said before. My friend and I turned our backs on him and kept walking. Then we heard footsteps. We knew he was running toward us. We stopped and turned around to face him. Within seconds he caught up to us, and while gasping for breath again, "You looking for Levon? If so, he deals out of the back now." My friend and I both knew he was under the assumption we were trying to buy drugs. We told him we were trying to get some tacos but the taco spot was closed.

He then asked what we were doing outside on this hot day. I told him, "We're actually out here trying to share the good news of Jesus, bro. What are your thoughts about God?" Surprised by my response, he paused and then said, "Oh man, I know God saved me!" Without wasting a moment, I responded, "That's a blessing! Could you do me a favor then, since you said God saved you?" He nodded his head in agreement and then I asked him, "Since you said God saved you, could you share the gospel with my friend and I before we head to our destination?" He looked puzzled and said, "The gospel?" Seeing that I had his attention I said, "Yes, the gospel. It's the message we hear that compels us to ask God to save us. Since you said God saved you, please share with us the message you heard when you realized you needed to ask God to save you."

He shook his head and told me he didn't know what I was talking about. Then I simply walked him through the G.O.S.P.E.L. acronym. When I got to the end, he said he had one question for me. Then his body language changed and he squared up as if he were going to punch me.

"You said that if I'm a sinner, I'm not good with God, so I'm asking you, am I good with God?"

I told him again that the gospel describes us as born in sin, and dead in it. The only way we can be good with God is by hearing the gospel, embracing Jesus as Savior, and taking the plea bargain He offers us. If we do not do this, then *no*—we are not good with God.

Leaning in closer to me, he clarified his question one more time: "So you're saying, if I haven't embraced Jesus then I am not good with God?" Looking directly at him, all the while anticipating him to take a swing at me, I said, "Yes, that's what I'm saying."

He stepped back and stood still for a moment.

Tears began to well up and eventually streamed down his face. I couldn't tell if he was crying because he was angry or if God was working on his heart. Turns out, it was both.

He told my friend and me that he was just released from prison a few months ago. He was homeless, and some nights he slept on his mother's couch. Doctors had diagnosed him with stage 4 pancreatic cancer and gave him a few months to live. After receiving the news a month ago, he had prayed the same prayer every day: "God, I'm going to meet You soon. If I am good with You, send someone to let me know. If I am not good with You, *send someone to let me know.*"

Surprised by his candid openness, I stood still, waiting to hear what he would say next.

"I kept asking you if I was good with God, because I couldn't believe my prayer was being answered. Now that you have told me I am not good with God, I have to ask, what must I do to be saved?"

As soon as he finished his sentence, my friend and I began to cry. We realized God's power was being put on display right before our eyes! We prayed with him as he admitted he was a sinner, he believed what Jesus did for him, and confessed Jesus as his Savior. After we prayed, we hugged each other. We talked for a little while and before we parted ways I asked, "Isn't it amazing that you kept pressing me by asking who I was looking for, when the entire time, God connected our lives so that I would be able to introduce you to the one you were looking for?" We all smiled at this fact.

Your final destination can be with God, living in the city He has created for all those who have taken His plea bargain. This city will be populated by men and women from various cultures, ethnicities, and social classes. God desires to put His power on display by saving you. So my question for you is, will you accept or reject His offer?

AFTERWORD

In 2010 I traveled to Atlanta to meet with Miguel Davila of ReachLife Ministries, the nonprofit arm of Reach Records. As we talked, Miguel said that greatest need for our generation was a resource that answered the simple question, "What is the gospel?" He challenged me to write a short book that could be understood by the hip hop and urban fanbase of the Unashamed movement.

On the flight back to Kansas City I brainstormed ways that I could accomplish this task. The result was a short, easy-to-read book, which also led to a CD that expressed the book's content in lyrical form. A couple months later I was asked to preach at the Legacy Conference hosted by Moody Bible Institute in Chicago. During my sermon I mentioned that our generation shouldn't be upset that the heroes of our faith (men like John Piper) are not creating resources contextualized to our reality in urban cities. I said that we need to develop our own resources.

After preaching I was approached by a man who wanted to ask me about my sermon comment. We met for lunch and he asked if I had any of these resources written. So I told him about my finished manuscript and offered to send it to him. That man's name was Barnabas Piper, son of the very John Piper I mentioned in my sermon. Barnabas took my manuscript and he told me he would submit a proposal to Moody Publishers. So on January 1, 2012, Moody Publishers released the first edition of G.O.S.P.E.L.

In the years since then I have received countless of emails, phone calls, and text messages that express gratitude for the way G.O.S.P.E.L. was written. I had merged hip-hop cultural references and slang with theological explanations (what I call *thebonics*). The easy-to-remember G.O.S.P.E.L. acronym provided saints around the globe with opportunities to share the gospel with marginalized communities.

Our modern-day slang becomes outdated very quickly, so a few years ago I felt a stirring in my heart from the Lord to revise the G.O.S.P.E.L. book. I wanted a more conceptual approach to sharing the gospel, and I wanted to aim the book at unbelievers (instead of a resource for believers). After taking time to pray, I contacted Moody Publishers and asked if we could revise G.O.S.P.E.L. I wanted to focus on communicating the gospel message to those who are not following Jesus.

This book is for you! If you do not yet know Jesus

Christ, you will be challenged by God's story and the gospel theme that is woven throughout it. The G.O.S.P.E.L. acronym will explain concepts in ways that you can understand. It is my prayer that God will guide your journey to find the truth—God's truth—that explains how to have a right relationship with Him. I pray you think deeply about what you read. The gospel bridge connects your story to God's story. I hope you will consider this message and find the eternal hope it provides.

NOTES

1. "Netflix Gets 16 Million Thanks to Lockdown," BBC News, April 21, 2020, www.bbc.com/news/business-52376022; "Bible Reading Drops During Social Distancing," *Christianity Today*, July 22, 2020, www.christianitytoday.com/news/2020/july/state-of-bible-reading-coronavirus-barna-abs.html.

2. I explain this point in chapter 1 of my book *Intensional: Kingdom Ethnicity in a Divided World* (Colorado Springs, CO: NavPress, 2019).

3. "How Courts Work," American Bar Association, September 9, 2019, https://www.americanbar.org/groups/public_education/resources/law_related_education_network/how_courts_work/pleabargaining.

SYSTEMATIC THEOLOGY FOR
THE URBAN CONTEXT

DNA: Foundations of the Faith presents each reader with a survey of systematic theology written in the heart language of the urban context. D.A. Horton writes with a conviction that every believer should have the privilege of being equipped with a working knowledge of what the principle teachings of Christianity are. This tool can be used in any setting from the seminary classroom to the local street corner.

978-0-8024-2320-7 | also available as an eBook

In the sixteenth century, the church faced a doctrinal crisis. Today, the crisis is race.

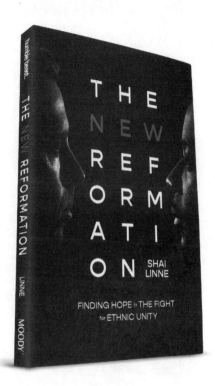

MOODY Publishers®

From the Word to Life®

We all know that racial unity is important. But how can Christians of different ethnicities pursue unity in an environment that is full of landmines on all sides? In *The New Reformation*, Christian hip-hop artist Shai Linne shows how the gospel applies to ethnic unity.

978-0-8024-2320-7
also available as eBook and audiobook

As those who know the Creator, Christians should be leading the way in creativity.

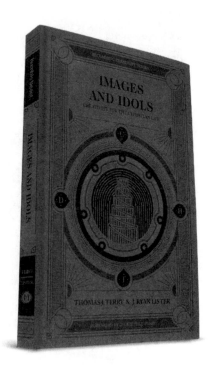

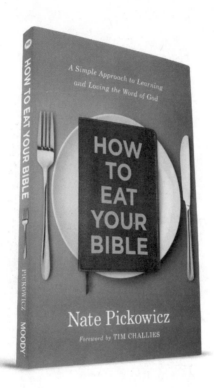